MATTER MOLECULES AND ATOMS

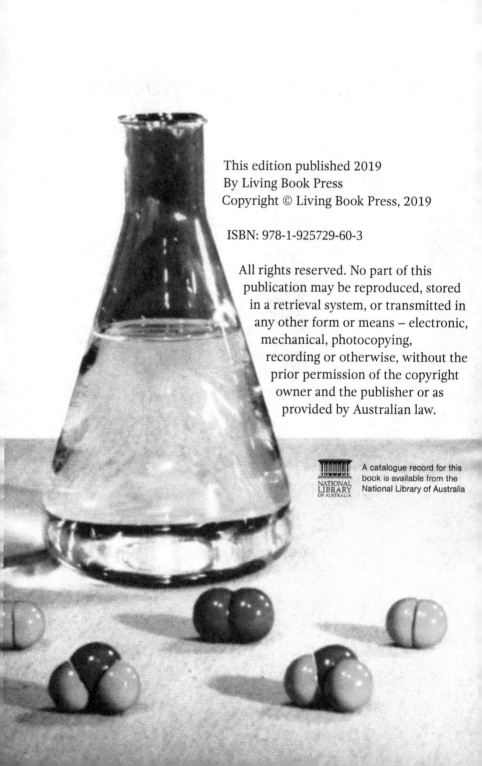

This edition published 2019
By Living Book Press
Copyright © Living Book Press, 2019

ISBN: 978-1-925729-60-3

A catalogue record for this
book is available from the
National Library of Australia

NATIONAL
LIBRARY
OF AUSTRALIA

Matter, Molecules, and Atoms

BERTHA MORRIS PARKER

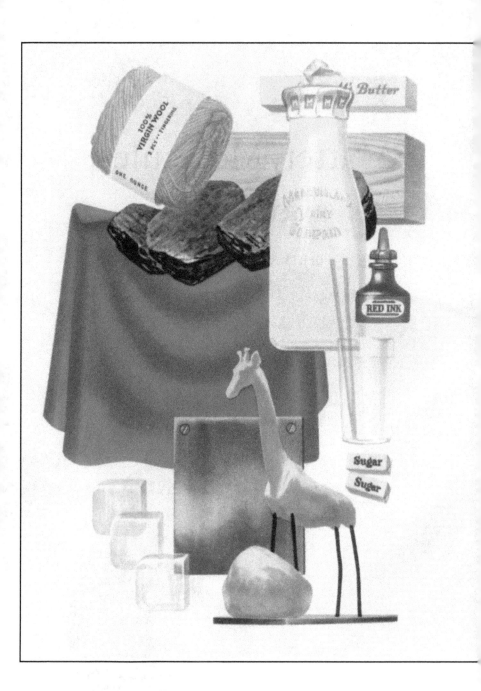

MATTER, MOLECULES, AND ATOMS

FOURTEEN different materials are pictured on page 2. It is not at all hard to tell these materials apart, for each one has certain characteristics, or properties; which make it unlike the others. Loaf sugar, for example, is hard, white, and sweet; it has no smell; it does not melt easily; it does dissolve easily in water. No other material pictured has this same combination of properties.

But, although each of the materials has properties of its own, all fourteen are alike in two ways: They all take up space. They all have weight.

All materials are alike in these same two ways. In fact, we define a material by saying that it is something which takes up space and has weight. Heat is not a material—it does not take up any space or weigh anything. Light is not a material—you could not measure it by the pint or the pound. Sound, radio waves, electric currents, and gravity are not materials, either.

It is easy to see that all the materials in the picture take up space. No one would expect to be able to pour milk into a glass already full of lemonade or to put an ice cube into the space occupied by a block of wood. It is not so easy to see that some materials—air, for example—take up space, but there are ways, some of which you will find later, of showing that they do.

Butter, sugar, and some of the other materials pictured are sold by the pound—it is clear that they weigh something. No one buys silk cloth or lemonade by the pound, but simply lifting these materials tells you that they have weight. In the case of air and some other materials, however, people were long in discovering that they, too, have weight.

All materials taken together may be spoken of as *matter*. We can now say, then, that every kind of matter takes up space and has weight.

SOLIDS, LIQUIDS, AND GASES

The materials pictured on page 2, although they can be told apart easily, can be grouped together in different ways. An important way in which some of them are different from the others is that some are solids while others are liquids. You do not have to be told that the milk, red ink, and lemonade are the liquids. The others are all solids.

A piece of any solid has a definite shape. A block of wood, for example, is the same shape whether it is on a table, in a beaker, or anywhere else. Of course, the shape of the block of wood could be changed. It could be carved into the figure of an animal. It could be ground into sawdust. It could be split into long, thin pieces. But it keeps its shape until something forces it into a different shape. And in some cases it takes a great deal of force to change the shape of a piece of solid material. Can you imagine tearing a silver dollar in two with your hands?

A piece of a solid material also has a size of its own. For this reason it is possible to buy 4 yards of silk cloth, or 2 square feet of copper, or wooden timbers 2 inches by 4 inches by 20 feet. There is no chance that a block of wood resting in a beaker will spread outward and upward to fill the whole beaker. There is no chance that piling other similar blocks on top of it will squeeze it into a much smaller space.

Solids do not, as many people think, have to be hard. Wool and silk and modeling clay are not hard, but they are solids. They are solids because they have a size and shape of their own.

Some solids occur in the form of beautifully shaped crystals. Quartz, for example, occurs in six-sided crystals that come to points at the ends. Snow crystals, with their six points, are well known to everyone.

Liquids do not have any definite shape. On a flat surface a liquid spreads out over the surface. In a container it takes the shape of the container.

But liquids do have a definite size. A quart of milk poured into another quart bottle will just fill it. Poured into a half-gallon bottle it will fill it exactly half full.

Probably, when you were thinking of which of the materials on page 2 were liquids and which solids, the question you asked yourself was: Which ones can be poured? All liquids can be poured. But of course sand and granulated sugar and flour can be poured, and they are solids. At first glance, it seems, moreover, that they have no shape of their own. Granulated sugar, if poured into a cup, will spread out to take the shape of the cup. But really the separate tiny little pieces of sugar—and of sand and of flour—have a shape of their own.

Most liquids are wet; that is, if you put your finger or a piece of paper into one, enough of the liquid would stick to your finger or the paper to make it wet. But there are exceptions. The liquid mercury, although it can be poured like water and although it takes the shape of a container just as water does, is not wet. If you stick your finger or a piece of paper into a bottle of mercury, it is just as dry as before.

The sketch below shows a surprising characteristic of liquids. In the experiment pictured, paper clips are dropped one at a time into a tumbler level full of water. More than a hundred clips can usually be dropped in before any water runs over the edge of the tumbler. Instead of overflowing, the water piles up. It acts very much as if there were a thin skin over the top. This characteristic of liquids is called *surface tension*. Perhaps you have heard of carrying water in a sieve. This is sometimes possible because of surface tension. It is sometimes possible, moreover, to make a needle float on water even though steel is heavier than water. Surface tension may keep it from sinking. Mercury shows surface tension even more clearly than water. Small bits of mercury are ball-shaped because of it.

Although all the materials pictured on page 2 are either solids or liquids, not all materials will fit into these two groups. Air is one that will not. Carbon dioxide, stove gas, hydrogen, and oxygen are others that will not. These materials are gases.

The left-hand picture on page 6 shows a way of making clear that air takes up space. The flask into which the boy is trying to pour colored water

looks empty but is really full of air. The air in the flask is holding the water out.

Gases have no shape of their own. It is ridiculous to think of making air into a model of a little animal. Gases take the shape of any container they are in. It is hard to see that they do, because most gases are invisible. There are, however, some colored gases that we can see. Various tests show that invisible gases take the shape of the containers they are in just as these colored gases do.

The right-hand picture at the top of the page also shows that air takes up space. It shows, too, another characteristic of air. The tumbler was full of air to begin with; and it was pushed straight down so that none of the air could escape. But there is now some water in the tumbler. The air has been squeezed into a smaller space.

A gas, unlike both liquids and solids, actually has no size of its own. If a quart bottle full of air were emptied into a really empty half-gallon bottle, the air would spread outward and upward to fill the whole space. Similarly, even if a space is full of air, a great deal more air can be squeezed into it. You see this happen with automobile tires all the time. Even though a tire is full of air, more air can be pumped in.

Every material is a liquid, a gas, or a solid. It is now clear that you have only two questions to ask about any material to find out which it is: Does it have a shape of its own? Does it have a size of its own? If the answer is yes to both of these questions, the material is a solid. If the answer is no to the first and yes to the second, the material is a liquid. If the answer is no to both, the material is a gas.

CHANGES OF STATE

Matter, you have seen, may be in solid, liquid, or gas form. Another way of saying the same thing is that there are three states of matter: solid, liquid, and gas.

When we say that a material is a solid, a liquid, or a gas, we usually mean that it is so at ordinary temperatures. But it is possible in many cases for gases to become liquids or solids, for liquids to become gases or solids, and for solids to become liquids or gases. Such changes are called *changes of state*.

Of all changes of state those that take place in water are probably most familiar to you. You know that water, a liquid, may change to ice, a solid, or to water vapor, a gas. You have seen ice change to a liquid, and you have seen the water vapor in the air change to drops of water on the outside of a pitcher of cold lemonade. Perhaps you do not know that water vapor can also change directly to a solid and that ice can change to water vapor without becoming a liquid on the way. Snowflakes are crystals of ice formed from water vapor, and in wintertime wet clothes hung out on the line may "freeze dry."

The changing of a liquid or solid to a gas is called *evaporation*. The word comes from "vapor," another word for gas. Some liquids evaporate faster than water. Alcohol, gasoline, and ether are among those that do. Dry ice is one of the solids you may have seen evaporate. It changes to a gas without changing to a liquid on the way. The left-hand picture on page 8 shows another solid changing to a gas. Crystals of iodine are changing to a violet vapor.

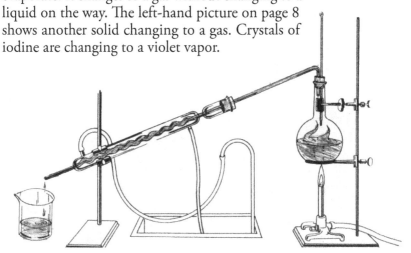

In many cases evaporation takes place merely from the surface of a liquid. But when a liquid is heated rapidly, bubbles of gas may form below the surface and then rise to the surface and break. We say then that the liquid is *boiling*. The water vapor that comes from boiling water has been given the name of "steam."

The changing of a solid to a liquid is called *melting*. In the right-hand picture above, the paraffin of the candle is melting and traveling up the wick. Butter, lard, sugar, iron, copper, and lead are among the other solids that melt.

The changing of a liquid or a gas to a solid is called *freezing*. Dry ice is made by freezing carbon dioxide, one of the gases in the air. Granite, a common rock, is formed by the freezing of hot, liquid rock from deep in the earth.

The changing of a gas to a liquid is called *condensation*. The changing of a gas to a solid may be called condensation, too, instead of freezing. Thus, when the water vapor of the air changes to snow crystals, we may say either that the water vapor condenses as snow crystals or that it freezes.

In any change of state a transfer of heat takes place. A material freezes or condenses only when it loses heat. Evaporation and melting mean a gain in heat.

Changes of state are of great practical importance. The diagram below shows one of the many uses to which we put them. Water is being distilled to rid it of mud and other impurities. The water is first heated to boiling. The steam passes through a condensing tube. There it is cooled by cold water flowing around it and is changed back to water. Since the mud and minerals in the water do not change to gases at the temperature at which water boils, they are left behind.

PUZZLES TO EXPLAIN

But how are changes of state possible? How can water freeze, alcohol evaporate, and steam condense? What makes the differences between solids, liquids, and gases? Long ago people began to puzzle over these questions. There were other somewhat similar puzzling problems, too.

The girl in the right-hand picture below is adding crystals of copper sulfate to water. The crystals are bright blue. When looked through a microscope you would not be able to see any bits of the copper sulfate. But it is there, as you can tell from the blue color of the liquid.

You have watched sugar and probably many other materials dissolve. *Dissolving* is quite different from melting. A solid by itself may melt when heated. It cannot dissolve unless there is another material present to dissolve it.

By no means all solids will dissolve in water. Sand, for example, will not. You can easily find this out for yourself by using filter paper. Filter paper is porous paper through which water can go easily. If a solution of copper sulfate is poured into a funnel lined with filter paper, the liquid which comes through the filter paper is bright blue. The copper sulfate is still present in the water. But if a mixture of sand and water is poured into a funnel lined with filter paper, the water comes through, but the sand—exactly as much as you put in is left on the paper. None of it has dissolved.

Water can dissolve many solids. It can dissolve many gases, too. It is the best dissolver, or *solvent*, known. The water you drink is almost sure to have both air and minerals dissolved in it.

There are other good solvents, too. Alcohol, naphtha, and car-

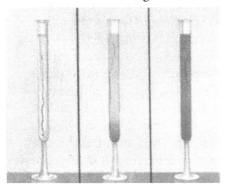 

bon tetrachloride are three of them. Each one of these can dissolve some materials which water cannot.

If you added some baking soda to water and found that it did not all disappear, it would not mean that baking soda did not dissolve in water. There is a limit to the amount of another material that a given amount of any liquid can dissolve.

But how can a solid or a gas dissolve in a liquid?

In the first diagram in the left-hand picture on page 9 a tiny crystal of potassium permanganate has been dropped into a test tube full of water. It is leaving a colored trail as it falls, because it is dissolving in the water. The second diagram shows the same test tube a day later. The third diagram shows the test tube a week later. Without being stirred, the potassium permanganate has spread all through the water. This experiment illustrates *diffusion*.

You are familiar with some examples of diffusion. The smell of onions cooking goes through a whole house. If a bottle of ether is opened in one corner of a closed room, some of it is soon in the opposite comer.

How does diffusion come about?

The pictures on these two pages show that changes in temperature may bring about changes in size. You have learned that solids and liquids have a size of their own. But this size changes somewhat with changes in temperature. The milk that fills one quart bottle will exactly fill any quart bottle if its temperature stays the same. But if its temperature is lowered, the milk will shrink, or contract, and will not quite fill the bottle. If, on the other hand, its temperature rises, it will expand, or grow larger, and more than fill a quart bottle. Many other solids and liquids expand when heated and contract when cooled.

The pictures on page 10 show that brass expands when heated. The ball when heated becomes too big to go through the ring.

Gases, too, expand when heated and contract when cooled. The early balloon pictured on this page rose when the air inside it was heated. The air expanded, and some of it escaped from the balloon. The balloon was then light enough to be pushed up by the surrounding air.

How is it possible for materials to expand and contract? A brass ball has no more brass in it when it is hot than when it is cold. Then how can it be bigger? How can a quart of milk swell to more than a quart when it is warmed and shrink to less than a quart when it is cooled? How can air change size with changes in temperature?

More than two thousand years ago Greek philosophers suggested a solution for these puzzles. Perhaps, they said, materials are made of tiny particles with spaces between. Their idea was more or less forgotten for a very long time, but it was the forerunner of our modern answer to the puzzles.

MOLECULES

In trying to solve the puzzling problems about which you have just been told, and other problems, too, scientists of the last century worked out this picture of matter: All materials are made up of unbelievably small particles, or molecules, which are always moving. In solids the molecules are packed so close together that each molecule keeps its position among the other molecules; it simply vibrates rapidly back and forth. In liquids the molecules are close together, but they move faster and much more freely than in solids. A molecule of a liquid does not keep its position among the other molecules of the liquid. In gases the molecules are far apart in comparison with their size, and they move very fast and very freely. As they move about they are continually bumping together and changing the direction in which they are going. The molecules of a material attract one another. The attraction is very slight in gases, much greater in liquids, and still greater in solids.

At first this picture of matter—the *molecular theory*, it is called—was questioned by many scientists. Molecules, if they existed, were far too small to be seen with even the strongest microscopes. But the theory explained so many happenings so well that all scientists came to accept it as true. And now, with the electron microscope, molecules of certain materials have actually been seen.

The nineteenth century ideas of molecules have had to be changed slightly in the case of some materials, but for our purposes those changes are not important. Let us see now how our puzzles can be explained in terms of molecules.

Solids keep their shape because their molecules attract one another with enough force to make them do so. In liquids and gases the attraction between the molecules is not strong enough to give liquids and gases a definite shape.

The attraction in liquids, however, is great enough to cause surface tension. The diagram below helps explain surface tension. A molecule below the surface of the liquid is pulled from all directions by the other molecules of the liquid. At the surface the pull of the other molecules is only from below. In the experiment pictured the pull is strong enough to allow the water to pile up for a considerable distance before it overflows.

The great attraction of the molecules in steel and wood and other similar solids for one another explains why pieces of these materials cannot easily be pulled apart. The speed with which the molecules of gases move, and their slight attraction for one another explain why gases have no definite size of their own. The molecules spread out to fill any space there is.

Gases can be compressed easily because there are big spaces between their molecules. The molecules of liquids and solids are already so close together that it is not easy to push them closer.

The expanding and contracting of materials when their temperatures change are easy to explain in terms of molecules. When a brass ball, for example, is heated, the molecules move faster and farther and the outermost molecules are pushed outward. The ball then takes up more space. When the ball is cooled, the molecules move less fast and far and the molecules are pulled closer together again. The ball gets smaller.

Changes of state are easily explained, too. When water evaporates, the water molecules simply move so far apart that the liquid becomes a gas. When steam condenses, the molecules move closer together. When iron melts, the molecules of iron move faster and more freely. When the molten iron freezes into solid iron again, the molecules have simply slowed down and stopped moving freely.

A lump of sugar put into a cup of water is separated into molecules. These molecules find their way in between the molecules of water. The sugar disappears because the separate molecules are much too small to be seen. Whenever anything dissolves, its particles go in between the particles of the material that dissolves it.

Diffusion is explained by the fact that molecules are always moving. When a bottle of ether is uncorked,

molecules of the ether move out between the molecules of air. In the experiment shown in the left-hand picture on page 9 molecule movement carries the potassium permanganate all through the water.

It is important that you do not get the idea that, because molecules are always moving, they are tiny living things. A molecule can move without being alive, just as a ball can fall to the ground without being alive. Living material is made of molecules, however, just as other materials are. You yourself are made of molecules.

Molecules of different substances are different in size. Most of them are much smaller than those that have been seen with an electron microscope. The molecules which make up air, for example, are so small that you breathe in billions of billions of them every time you breathe—hundreds of times as many as you could have counted if you had been alive ever since the world began and had been counting every minute of your life. It is a great strain on the imagination to try to picture the very small size of the molecules and the enormous number of these tiny particles in any sizable amount of any material.

PHYSICAL AND CHEMICAL CHANGES

When a lump of sugar is dissolved in water, it keeps enough of its properties for us to recognize it. Although it is no longer hard and white, it can still be recognized by its sweet taste. Moreover, the water can be made to evaporate and leave the sugar behind, hard and white just as it was at first. The sugar is sugar all the while. A piece of paper can be torn into tiny bits, but each piece is still paper. When mercury is frozen, as it can be, in dry ice, it becomes hard, but it remains the same silvery metal. Such changes as these are called *physical changes*.

The distilling of water, pictured on page 8, is a series of physical changes. The water becomes warmer—one physical change; it evaporates—a second change; the vapor becomes cooler—a third change; and, as a final change, the vapor condenses. The changing of iodine crystals to iodine vapor, pictured on page 8, is a physical change. The changes pictured on pages 9, 10, and 14 are physical changes, too.

The pictures on page 14 show two of the steps in making a glass flask. The first workman is blowing a lump of hot, soft glass into the desired shape. The second workman is cutting off the flask. In the end the glass is cold and hard instead of hot and soft, and the flask is not the shape of the lump of glass. But the glass is glass still.

Dissolving, change in temperature, expansion and contraction, changes of state, changes in shape, and the dividing up of a piece of material into two or more pieces are always physical changes. Compressing air, as you do when you force it into an automobile tire, rubbing out a pencil mark with an eraser, mixing coloring

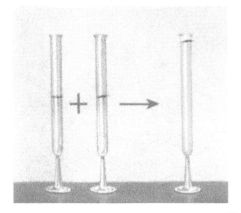

matter with margarine, taking the mud out of water by filtering it, and beating white of egg until it is stiff are other examples of physical change. In none of these changes is any material produced which was not there in the beginning.

In physical changes the molecules of a substance may move farther apart. They may move closer together. They may find their way in between the molecules of another substance. The molecules of one substance may be separated from those of another. But the molecules themselves continue to be the same as in the beginning.

Some changes, however, are very different. The pictures on page 15 show two such changes.

In the left-hand picture two colorless solutions are put together. Fine particles of a bright-yellow solid are formed. There are so many of them that they make the whole mixture look yellow. Here a new material has been formed—a material with properties different from those of either of the chemicals that were mixed together. There are now molecules that are unlike the molecules of the materials that were mixed. A change of this kind is a *chemical change*.

The right-hand picture also shows a chemical change. Here vinegar is being added to a solution of baking soda and water. Bubbles of carbon dioxide are making the mixture foam. The carbon dioxide is very different from the vinegar, the baking soda, and the water. Here again a new material is being produced—the sign of a chemical change.

THE BEGINNINGS OF CHEMISTRY

Thousands of years ago people learned how to bring about some kinds of chemical changes that were very helpful to them. They did not understand how the changes were brought about, but they knew that in the end they had materials quite different from those they started with. They learned, for example, how to change wood to charcoal. They learned how to get iron by heating a certain kind of red rock with charcoal. Another of their many similar discoveries was that, if dough was allowed to stand, bubbles of gas would form in it and make it rise. The bread made by baking the dough would be light.

For a long time no one was very much concerned about how such changes could be explained. They were simply interested in getting the resulting products.

But more than two thousand years ago the learned men of Greece became interested in the whys of such changes just as they were interested in the whys of physical changes. Aristotle, a famous Greek philosopher, came to the conclusion that all matter was made of four elements: fire, air, earth, and water. One material could be changed to another, he thought, by taking away one or more of these elements or by adding one or more of them.

Since the Greeks took the first steps in finding out what things are made of, we can say that chemistry began with them. But they did nothing but talk about their ideas. The Egyptians of a few centuries later, however, thought that they might be able to put the Greek ideas to use. Perhaps by finding out how to add or subtract elements they could bring about new and helpful changes in materia}s. Perhaps they might find a way of changing iron and

other cheap metals into gold. Nothing came of their attempts.

But the idea of changing other metals into gold did not die. More than a thousand years ago the Arabs took up the search. They gave their studies a name, alchemy.

Alchemy flourished in Europe in the Middle Ages. Europe's alchemists continued to hunt for a way of changing other metals into gold. They also hunted for a so-called "philosopher's stone" that would give its wearer eternal youth. The alchemists' work was cloaked in mystery. They used a great many mystic symbols that no one but they themselves could understand. Some alchemists were really trying to find out whether Aristotle's elements were the building stones of matter. But so many claims of the alchemists were fraudulent that alchemy came to have a bad reputation.

The alchemists did, however, make some helpful discoveries. They discovered some new metals and some new drugs and other chemicals. They designed apparatus that helped them study materials. From their work there came, too, the idea that there are elements out of which all materials are made, but that, instead of being air, earth, fire, and water, they are such things as sulfur, iron, mercury, and gold. When alchemy was turned away from a hunt for gold and the philosopher's stone to experiments which would find out more about the building blocks of matter, modern chemistry began.

ELEMENTS, COMPOUNDS, MIXTURES

The chemists of today tell us that there are about a hundred simple substances, or *elements*, out of which all matter is made. All other materials are either *compounds* of two or more elements, or *mixtures*.

Some elements are very, very rare. Others are so common that they are known to almost everyone. Listed below are fifty of the elements. After the name of each one is given the symbol, or sign, which chemists use for it.

SULFUR

CARBON

IODINE

Aluminum	Al	Magnesium	Mg
Antimony	Sb	Manganese	Mn
Argon	A	Mercury	Hg
Arsenic	As	Molybdenum	Mo
Barium	Ba	Neon	Ne
Bismuth	Bi	Nickel	Ni
Boron	B	Nitrogen	N
Bromine	Br	Oxygen	0
Calcium	Ca	Phosphorus	P
Carbon	C	Platinum	Pt
Cesium	Cs	Potassium	K
Chlorine	Cl	Radium	Ra
Chromium	Cr	Radon	Rn
Cobalt	Co	Selenium	Se
Copper	Cu	Silicon	Si
Fluorine	F	Silver	Ag
Gold	Au	Sodium	Na
Helium	He	Strontium	Sr
Hydrogen	H	Sulfur	S
Iodine	I	Tin	Sn
Iridium	Ir	Titanium	Ti
Iron	Fe	Tungsten	W
Krypton	Kr	Uranium	U
Lead	Pb	Vanadium	V
Lithium	Li	Zinc	Zn

NICKEL NITRATE

LEAD OXIDE

MANGANESE DIOXIDE

Until recently chemists thought that there were only 92 elements. There are only 92 natural elements. But scientists in their laboratories have produced others. By the end of 1956 they had produced neptunium, plutonium, americium, curium, berkelium, californium, einsteinium, fermium, and mendelevium. Four of these new elements were named for famous scientists. The others were named for planets or places.

Three common elements are pictured at the top of page 19. From this picture you should not get the idea that all elements are solids. They are not. Two, mercury and bromine, are liquids. Oxygen, hydrogen, nitrogen, and several others are gases. Many of the solid elements and one of the liquid elements—mercury—are metals.

In a compound, elements are joined together to form a material quite different from the elements it is made of. Water is one of the commonest compounds. It is composed of oxygen and hydrogen, two gases. Table salt is a compound of chlorine, a poisonous greenish gas, and sodium, a poisonous metal.

Like elements, compounds may be gases, liquids, or solids. In fact, you cannot tell by a material's appearance whether it is an element or a compound. You would not know from the pictures of the compounds on page 19 that they are not elements. Not even with the strongest microscope can you see in a compound the different elements of which it is made.

The chemical names of the compounds in the picture are given in the legends. Every compound has a chemical name which gives a clue as to what it is made of. Manganese dioxide is made of manganese and oxygen, lead oxide of lead and oxygen. The nickel nitrate is made of nickel, nitrogen, and, as the "ate" indicates, oxygen. Many compounds also have common names just as water and salt have.

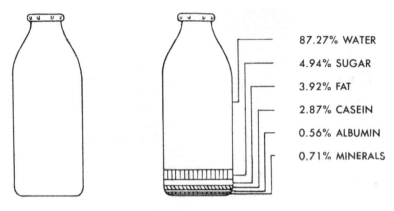

87.27% WATER

4.94% SUGAR

3.92% FAT

2.87% CASEIN

0.56% ALBUMIN

0.71% MINERALS

There are many, many thousands of compounds. No one could ever give an exact figure because chemists so frequently find new ways of combining elements to make new compounds.

A mixture may be a mixture of two or more elements. It may be a mixture of two or more compounds. It may be a mixture of one or more elements with one or more compounds.

Air is one of the most common mixtures. It is a mixture of several elements—:nitrogen, oxygen, argon, krypton, and neon among others—with carbon dioxide, a compound. There is always some water vapor in the air, too. The pictures on these two pages show four other common mixtures. These mixtures are all mixtures of compounds. When we make butter we are separating the fat from the other compounds in milk. When we make cheese we are taking out the casein and albumin.

Among the most valuable mixtures are the alloys—mixtures of metals. Brass (a mixture of copper and zinc), bronze (copper and tin), and steel (iron, carbon, and often another metal) are the most common.

In some cases the separate materials in a mixture can be seen. But this is not true of all mixtures. Solutions are mixtures, and, as you know, dissolved materials are often completely lost to view.

Since air, milk, and steel have been mentioned as mixtures, it is clear that mixtures, like elements and compounds, may be solids, liquids, or gases.

There is no limit to the number of different mixtures that can be made. By far the greatest number of the materials around us are mixtures. Of the materials pictured on page 2, there is only one pure element—copper. Only the sugar and the ice (if it was made of distilled water) are pure compounds. All the others are mixtures.

ATOMS

The theory of molecules explained physical changes. It did not give a clear picture of how an element, a compound, and a mixture differ. It did not explain, either, how chemical changes come about. To answer these questions scientists worked out the *atomic theory.*

The smallest particle of any element, according to this theory, is an atom. Molecules are built of atoms. A molecule may be made of only one atom; it may on the other hand be made of many. In the molecule of an element all the atoms, if there are more than one, are atoms of that element. A molecule of oxygen, for example, is made up of two atoms of oxygen. But in a molecule of a compound there are atoms of at least two kinds. Every molecule of a compound must therefore have at least two atoms in it.

No one has ever seen an atom. This is not surprising since only the largest molecules can be seen even with the electron microscope. But the atomic theory, like the molecular theory, explains so many happenings so well that now no scientists doubt it. Scientists now believe they know, moreover, much about how atoms are joined together to form molecules.

On these pages four compounds are pictured and their formulas given. The formula for a compound tells what kinds of atoms and how many of each there are in a molecule of the compound. NaCl is common salt, or sodium chloride. The symbol scientists use for an element stands for one atom of the element. A molecule of salt is, then, made of

NaCl

SiO$_2$

one atom of sodium and one of chlorine. SiO_2 is quartz, or silicon dioxide. For every atom of silicon there are two of oxygen. CCl_4 is carbon tetrachloride, a common cleaning fluid. In every molecule of this material there are four atoms of chlorine and one of carbon. HgO is mercuric oxide, commonly called red oxide of mercury. As you see from its formula, there is in it one atom of oxygen for every one of mercury.

The formula for water is H_2O. Below are the formulas for a few of the many thousands of other compounds.

Baking soda	$NaHCO_3$
Starch	$C_6H_{10}O_5$
Cane Sugar	$C_{12}H_{22}O_{11}$
Vinegar	CH_3COOH
Carbon dioxide	CO_2
Grain alcohol	C_2H_5OH
Copper sulfate	$CuSO_4$
Marble	$CaCO_3$

A formula like CH_3COOH may surprise you. You may wonder why it is not written $C_2H_4O_2$. Chemists write it as they do to tell something about the way the atoms are joined together in each molecule.

In a compound, although each molecule is made of more than one kind of atom, the molecules are alike. In a mixture there are at least two different kinds of molecules. The diagrams on page 24 will help make this difference clear.

How does the atomic theory explain the puzzle of chemical change? When a chemical change takes place, there is, according to the theory, a regrouping of atoms. Molecules of one or more new materials are formed in the regrouping.

CCl_4

HgO

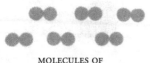

MOLECULES OF
AN ELEMENT

MOLECULES OF
ANOTHER ELEMENT

A MIXTURE OF
THESE ELEMENTS

A COMPOUND OF THESE ELEMENTS

A MIXTURE OF
TWO COMPOUNDS

A MIXTURE OF
TWO ELEMENTS
AND A COMPOUND

Suppose, for example, a little red oxide of mercury (HgO) is heated in a test tube. It is broken up into the elements it is made of. The atom of oxygen in each molecule breaks away from the atom of mercury and joins the atom of oxygen from another molecule to form a molecule of oxygen. The molecules of oxygen escape from the test tube. The molecules of mercury are left behind. Here is the chemist's shorthand way of telling what happens:

$$2HgO \rightarrow 2Hg + O_2$$

In some chemical changes atoms of two elements join to form molecules of a compound. When powdered iron and powdered sulfur are mixed together and heated, the atoms of iron join the atoms of sulfur to form iron sulfide. Here is the story in the chemist's language:

$$Fe + S \rightarrow FeS$$

The chemical changes pictured on page 15 are more complicated. Here is the story of what happens in the experiment in the left-hand picture:

$$HgCl_2 + 2NaOH \rightarrow Hg(OH)_2 + 2NaCl$$
(mercuric (sodium (mercuric (sodium
chloride) hydroxide) hydroxide) chloride)

The yellow solid is the mercuric hydroxide. Do you see that in this change there is a change of chemical partners?

When vinegar is added to baking soda, this happens:

$$NaHCO_3 + CH_3COOH \rightarrow CO_2 + CH_3COONa + H_2O$$

It would take books and books to tell of all the chemical changes that go on about us. Knowing about atoms helps explain each one of them.

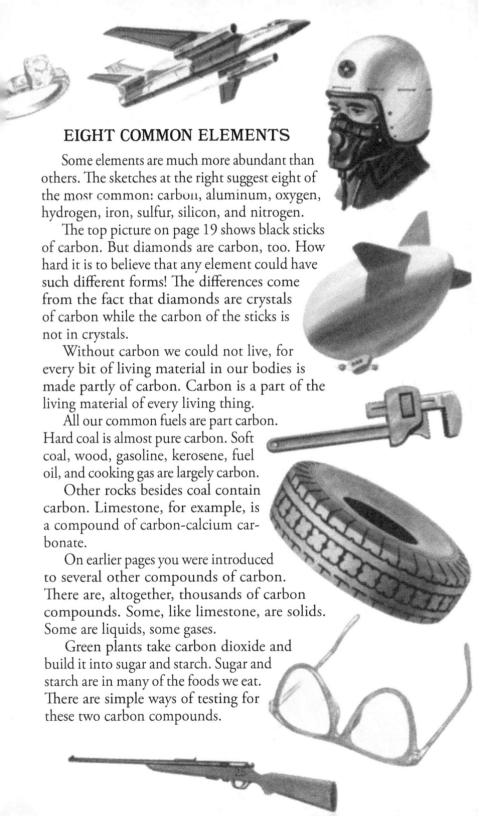

EIGHT COMMON ELEMENTS

Some elements are much more abundant than others. The sketches at the right suggest eight of the most common: carbon, aluminum, oxygen, hydrogen, iron, sulfur, silicon, and nitrogen.

The top picture on page 19 shows black sticks of carbon. But diamonds are carbon, too. How hard it is to believe that any element could have such different forms! The differences come from the fact that diamonds are crystals of carbon while the carbon of the sticks is not in crystals.

Without carbon we could not live, for every bit of living material in our bodies is made partly of carbon. Carbon is a part of the living material of every living thing.

All our common fuels are part carbon. Hard coal is almost pure carbon. Soft coal, wood, gasoline, kerosene, fuel oil, and cooking gas are largely carbon.

Other rocks besides coal contain carbon. Limestone, for example, is a compound of carbon-calcium carbonate.

On earlier pages you were introduced to several other compounds of carbon. There are, altogether, thousands of carbon compounds. Some, like limestone, are solids. Some are liquids, some gases.

Green plants take carbon dioxide and build it into sugar and starch. Sugar and starch are in many of the foods we eat. There are simple ways of testing for these two carbon compounds.

The right-hand picture on page 27 shows the test for starch. When a drop of iodine is added to anything containing starch, a purple color appears—the sign that starch is present.

The right-hand picture on page 29 shows a test for certain kinds of sugar. Fehling's solution, a mixture of several compounds, is used for the testing. It comes in two parts, A and B. To test a food for sugar, add equal amounts of solutions A and B. Heat the mixture. If an orange color results, sugar is present.

Aluminum is the most abundant of all the metals on earth. Before the nineteenth century, however, no one had ever seen it. It occurs in nature only in compounds. Many rocks and all clays contain it. The finding of a cheap way of separating aluminum from some of its compounds is one of the triumphs of modern science.

Aluminum has played an important part in the advance of aviation. It is light and does not rust. Aluminum foil and aluminum pans are much used in cooking.

Oxygen is the commonest of all the elements. The air is about one-fifth oxygen. Water, by weight, is eight-ninths oxygen. The oxygen in the earth's crust weighs as much as all the other elements put together. You yourself are more than half oxygen. There is oxygen in almost everything around you.

The oxygen in water, in rocks, and in your body is joined with other elements to form compounds. In air, on the other hand, much of the oxygen is free, that is, not in a compound.

Free oxygen is necessary for burning. For this reason fires must have a constant supply of air. We have to breathe free oxygen in order to live. Otherwise the food we eat cannot burn in our bodies and furnish us with the energy we have to have. Flyers who go high above the earth, where the air is thin, carry tanks of oxygen with them.

It is not easy to get pure oxygen by separating it from the other gases in the air. Oxygen can, however, be obtained from some of its compounds quite easily. The sketch at the bottom of the page shows one way of doing so. The material in the test tube is a mixture of two chemicals: potassium chlorate ($KClO_3$) and manganese

dioxide (MnO_2). Heating the mixture drives off the oxygen from the potassium chlorate. The oxygen bubbles up into the bottle full of water and drives the water out. Hydrogen looks like oxygen—they are both invisible gases—but it has some properties that make it very different from oxygen. It is much lighter than oxygen—in fact, it is the lightest of all known substances. Because of its lightness, hydrogen was once much used in balloons. Now, however, helium is being substituted for it whenever possible, because hydrogen can be set on fire very easily.

There is little free hydrogen on the earth, but there are thousands of hydrogen compounds. It is hydrogen, you remember, which is combined with oxygen to form water. Hydrogen is one of the four most abundant elements in our bodies. It is one of the elements in sugar, starch, and many, many other compounds of carbon. Hydrogen is, moreover, always a part of the chemicals called *acids*.

"Acid" comes from the Latin word for "sour." All acids taste sour when they are weak. Vinegar, lemon juice, green apples, sour cherries, and grapefruit are all sour because they contain acids. And every one of the acids contains hydrogen.

Some acids are very strong. It would not be at all safe to taste them unless they were diluted with a great deal of water. On this page you are shown a safe way of testing for acids. The boy is using litmus paper—paper colored with a special kind of dye. Some litmus paper is pink; some is blue. In acids pink litmus paper stays pink and blue litmus paper turns pink.

Litmus paper can also be used to test for *bases*. Bases are the opposites of acids. In bases pink litmus paper turns blue and blue litmus paper stays blue. Bases always contain both oxygen and hydrogen. In the formula for a base there is always an OH. Lye

(NaOH) is a very strong base. Ammonium hydroxide (NH_4OH), formed when ammonia is dissolved in water, is a weak base.

Next to aluminum, iron is the most abundant metal. Thousands of years ago men found how to get iron rather easily from some of its ores. They began making tools of it. Later they learned to make it into steel. Much of the world's industry today depends on this metal.

The left-hand picture on page 29 shows four of the compounds in which iron occurs. Notice the different colors of the different compounds. They help you understand how hard it is to guess, from the look of a material, what elements it is made of. The grayish-black material is magnetite (Fe_3O_4), the red material, hematite (Fe_2O_3), the green, iron sulfate ($FeSO_4$), and the yellow, iron chloride ($FeCl_2$).

Sulfur is one of the elements pictured on page 19. Usually, as in the picture, sulfur is a yellow powder. It may be in the form of yellow crystals instead. It may also be a dark-brown rubbery substance. It can disguise itself just as carbon can.

You have already met two compounds of sulfur: copper sulfate and sulfuric acid. Sulfuric acid is the most important sulfur compound. It has many uses, among them making ammunition and fertilizer and getting gasoline from petroleum. This acid is sometimes called "the king of chemicals."

Sulfur itself used to be called burning stone, or brimstone, because it catches fire very easily. Because it is easy to set on fire it is used in making matches. Sulfur is also used in manufacturing things of rubber. Rubber was of very little importance until the discovery was made that sulfur could be used to keep it from being sticky in warm weather and stiff in cold weather. Then a great many uses—as a material for automobile tires, for example—were found for it.

Silicon is, next to oxygen, the most abundant element on earth. But you are almost sure never to have seen it. It occurs in nature only in compounds, just as aluminum does. You have already found that quartz is a compound of silicon. When you know that sand is made up mostly of tiny bits of quartz, it is clear that silicon is very abundant.

Most glass is made of sand. Glass plays an important part in our lives; silicon therefore does, too. Since the lenses of our glasses are made of glass, silicon may be helping you read this book.

Nitrogen is another element that we could not live without. All living material contains nitrogen just as it contains oxygen and hydrogen. You yourself, then, are part nitrogen.

Nitrogen, like hydrogen and oxygen, is a colorless gas. It is very abundant in the air—more than four-fifths of the air is made of it. The nitrogen our bodies must have in order to build the new living material needed for growth and repair does not, however, come from the air. It comes instead from some of the foods we eat. One reason why we need to eat such foods as milk, eggs, meat, and cheese is that they all contain nitrogen.

Nitrogen is not a very good "joiner." There are not nearly so many compounds of nitrogen as there are compounds of oxygen and hydrogen. Laughing gas, which you may have been given at the dentist's when you had a tooth pulled, is one compound of nitrogen. Nitric acid is another. Nitric acid, like sulfuric acid, is important in industry. Compounds of nitrogen are used in explosives. Explosives play an important part in building roads, mining coal, and other such everyday work as well as in waging war.

CONTROLLING CHEMICAL CHANGES

Chemical changes are brought about in various ways. Knowing how they are brought about lets us start them when we wish them to occur. It helps us prevent them or stop them if we do not wish them to go on.

The picture below shows a current of electricity bringing about a chemical change. The current from the dry cells is flowing through water to which a few drops of sulfuric acid have been added, and is breaking the water up into hydrogen and oxygen. The hydrogen is collecting in one tube, the oxygen in the other. Since in a molecule of water there are two atoms of hydrogen and only one of oxygen, twice as much hydrogen as oxygen comes from the water.

Many of the metal things we use are metal plated. Many silver spoons, for example, are silver only on the outside. Such spoons are made of brass or some other rather cheap metal and are then given a coating of silver. Electric currents are used to do metal plating. By flowing through solutions of metal compounds, they cause the metals from the compounds to be deposited on the things to be plated. It goes without saying that if you wished to plate anything with silver you would use a compound of silver; if you wished to plate anything with copper you would use a compound of copper; and so on.

Heat brings about many chemical changes. You have already found that it is possible to get oxygen by heating certain chemicals. You have found out, too, that heat may cause sulfur and iron to

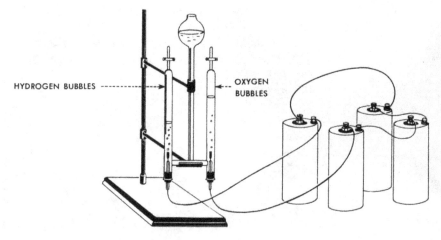

HYDROGEN BUBBLES

OXYGEN BUBBLES

join to form iron sulfide. In the picture at the bottom of page 32 heat is causing a chemical change in coal. It is producing a gas that will burn; coal tar, which is a liquid; and coke, which is a solid.

You have probably accidentally allowed heat to bring about chemical changes. Whenever food is scorched, a chemical change has taken place in it.

Heat starts fires to burning, and burning is one of our most important chemical changes. In starting a fire, heat starts the elements in the fuels to uniting with oxygen. New compounds are formed that are made up partly of oxygen. For example, when charcoal, which is carbon, burns, it unites with oxygen to form carbon dioxide (CO_2).

In many cases merely putting two materials together brings about a chemical change. The pictures on page 15 are examples of chemical changes brought about in this way. The pictures above show two other examples.

In the left-hand picture at the top of the page a boy is blowing his breath, which contains carbon dioxide, into limewater. Calcium carbonate, a white solid, is being formed. It makes the limewater look milky.

In the right-hand picture a girl is pouring a few drops of glycerin on a pile of powdered potassium permanganate. A chemical change at once begins to take place—one that produces so much heat that the mixture bursts into flame.

Since chemical changes may be started merely by the mixing of two materials, it is not wise to mix chemicals you know nothing about. Careless experimenting is dangerous.

Some chemical changes will not take place unless water is present. Baking powder is a mixture of baking soda and some acid material. So long as the mixture is dry, no change takes place in it.

But as soon as water is added, the molecules of the two materials break up and the parts join together in a different way to form new compounds. One of these is carbon dioxide. When baking powder is put into moist cake batter, bubbles of carbon dioxide form and puff the batter up.

Light brings about many chemical changes. Our very lives depend on chemical changes which light helps bring about in the leaves of green plants. It is light which enables green plants to make sugar and starch from water and carbon dioxide. The plants are then able to make other foods from the starch and sugar. If green plants did not make food, we could not live, for we get all our food either directly or indirectly from them.

Other chemical changes brought about by light account for much of the fading of colored materials. Light brings about a chemical change in many dyes.

Still other chemical changes produced by light make possible the taking of pictures. The chemical changes take place in the chemicals with which the film is coated.

Blueprints are among the simplest kinds of pictures made by chemical changes. Blueprint paper is coated with a chemical sensitive to light, that is, a chemical in which light will bring about changes. The paper looks pale green, as in the top picture on page 33. The chemical will dissolve in water. If the paper is washed, all the coating will wash off and leave nothing but clear white paper.

But if a piece of fresh blueprint paper is exposed to light, chemical changes bring about a change in color. At the same time the coating becomes insoluble in water. When the paper is washed, it is clear dark blue.

A blueprint like the one in the bottom picture on page 33 is made in this way: A leaf is laid on a piece of fresh blueprint paper. Then the paper with the leaf on it is held in sunlight for a short time. Light strikes the paper where the leaf does not cover it. It changes the chemical there. The chemical under the leaf remains unchanged or at least is changed very little. When the paper is washed, a white or pale-blue picture of the leaf is left on a dark-blue background.

Certain chemicals, without changing

themselves, speed up the changes in other materials. You remember that, in generating oxygen, manganese dioxide was put with the potassium chlorate. The heat of the flame drove oxygen from the potassium chlorate; it did not change the manganese dioxide. But unless the manganese dioxide is present it is very hard to drive the oxygen from the potassium chlorate. There are many other materials that act like manganese dioxide. We have a number of them in our own bodies. We have some, for example, which help digest the food we eat. Chemicals which help bring about changes in other materials without being changed themselves are called *catalysts*.

Food is often spoiled by very tiny plants which grow in it. The plants—bacteria, yeasts, and molds—bring about chemical changes in the foods. Yeasts, for example, break up sugar into alcohol and carbon dioxide. Sometimes extremely poisonous compounds are produced when bacteria grow in food.

It is easy to see how some chemical changes can be prevented. Materials in which heat is likely to bring about an undesirable chemical change can be kept cool. Materials sensitive to light can be protected from it.

33

Materials which change when they are mixed can be kept apart.

Materials which change when moist can be kept dry. It goes without saying that to prevent currents of electricity from bringing about chemical changes in a material one has only to see that no electric currents flow through the material. Many ways have been found of checking the growth of bacteria, yeasts, and molds and thus lessening the amount of damage to foods. Among the ways of checking their growth are drying foods, freezing them, canning them, keeping them cold, and preserving them with salt or sugar.

But of course we do not wish to stop all chemical changes. As you have already found out, stopping some of the chemical changes that go on in us and round about us would make it impossible for us to live.

ATOMS AT WORK

The time we are living in is often called the atomic age. The atomic age began when scientists discovered that enormous amounts of energy could be got by splitting atoms.

Having found out that all substances are built of atoms, scientists wanted to know what atoms themselves are like. Queerly enough, it took big machines, or "atom smashers," such as the cyclotron to explore tiny atoms.

It goes without saying that atoms of different elements are different. The very simplest atom is the hydrogen atom. It is made, scientists believe, of a tiny particle called an *electron* which travels at unbelievable speed around a larger, heavier *nucleus*. The nucleus is a particle called a *proton*.

The atoms of every element are made of electrons traveling around nuclei. But in every element except hydrogen each atom has more than one electron. And the nucleus of every other kind of

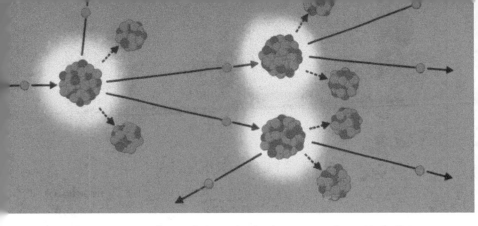

atom is more complicated than the hydrogen nucleus. In helium, for instance, the nucleus is made of two protons and two particles called *neutrons*. Two electrons circle around it. Uranium has 92 protons and 146 neutrons in its nucleus and has 92 electrons. But even a uranium atom is largely empty space.

Splitting an atom means splitting the nucleus. For this reason atomic energy is often called nuclear energy.

An atom was first split in 1938. Three years later a way was found of using the splitting of one atom to set off the splitting of other atoms. The idea was first used in the atomic bomb. Billions of atoms were split in less than a second, and the amount of energy turned loose did terrific damage. Now ways have been found of controlling the splitting of atoms. They can be made to supply a steady amount of energy.

Atomic energy is being put to many peacetime uses. Uranium is the atomic fuel used most often. Atomic-powered electric power plants are being built. Submarines are being driven by atomic energy. Before long it is likely that big ocean liners and rockets for exploring outer space will be driven by it. It promises to unlock many secrets for scientists. And great areas of the world now unfit for people may be made livable by the putting of atoms to work.

Energy can also be got by making hydrogen atoms fuse together. But the energy from fusion has not yet been tamed.

SEE FOR YOURSELF

1. The picture above shows the models of three molecules of one of the compounds pictured on pages 22 and 23. Which compound is it? Out of colored modeling clay make similar models of the molecules of other elements and compounds. Be sure to use a different color for each element.

2. Try for yourself as many as you can of the experiments pictured in this book.

3. Watch water boil in a glass flask or beaker. Where do the bubbles form?

4. Find out which of these liquids evaporates fastest: ether, alcohol, glycerin.

5. Get some dry ice. See for yourself that this solid evaporates without first melting.

6. Find out whether sugar dissolves faster in hot water or in cold water.

7. Make a collection of elements.

8. Find out how many of the compounds on the shelves of your science room contain oxygen.

9. Make a blueprint.

10. Copperplate some small metal object. Search the internet to find out how.

11. The opposite page shows five models of molecules and a flask containing water. Two of the molecules are water. What are the three others?

12. Notice the liquids in the flasks pictured on the inside front cover. Beside each flask there is a model of a molecule of the material in the flask. Do the liquids look alike? Are the models alike? What conclusion can you draw?

CPSIA information can be obtained
at www.ICGtesting.com
Printed in the USA
BVHW060757170720
583807BV00001B/27